YOUR PROMOTION IS IN MOTION!

By

Greg Mauro

8/21/99

Dear Jill,
Thank you from
always being a voice of
for encouragement in my & Teri's
lives - love and appreciate
you & Merlin much!
Love & prayers,
Greg

SEVEN GAME CHANGING WORDS FROM GOD
THAT WILL PROMOTE YOU TO YOUR
GREATER DESTINY

DEDICATION

My life and destiny were forever changed in 1987, when as a graduating student at Oral Roberts University, God called me to stand by the side of Morris and Theresa Cerullo.

This message would not be possible apart from the privilege and impartation I have received serving over three decades with a front row seat to one of the greatest pioneers in church history, my mentor and spiritual father, Dr. Morris Cerullo.

Dr. Cerullo's life and message is not a message of comfortable Christianity. It is a message of purposeful Christianity.

The example – the impartation – the message – of Morris Cerullo's life and influence permeates each page you are about to read that will take you behind the scenes of God's personal dealings and impartation in my own season of transition.

With a heart overflowing with gratitude, love and honor, I humbly dedicate "Your Promotion is In Motion" to the incredible lives, ministry, influence and legacy of Morris and Theresa Cerullo and pray God will use it to continue building His army.

I also dedicate this message to my great praying mother, Barbara and my incredible partner in life, love and ministry: my beautiful wife, Jeri and our eight amazing children, their spouses and nine wonderful grandchildren who are a daily reminder of the goodness and blessing of God.

WHAT KEY LEADERS ARE SAYING ABOUT
"YOUR PROMOTION IS IN MOTION"

"Greg Mauro is a 21st Century Elisha, called by God to stand by Morris and Theresa Cerullo. God has elevated him to levels he never imagined or aspired, seeking only to serve. I know of no one who is as qualified to write, *Your Promotion is in Motion* as Pastor Greg. It is life changing and a must read."

Pastor Tommy Barnett,
Co-Pastor, Dream City Church

"In *Your Promotion Is In Motion*, Greg Mauro shares seven powerful nuggets of revelation and empowerment from a heart of proven faithfulness and dedication.

Greg has served the ministry and the anointing of one of God's greatest generals, Dr. Morris Cerullo for over three decades and has learned a thing or two about favor and promotion.

Your Promotion Is In Motion will break you through into your "Greater Destiny" - one of favor and promotion! Get your copy today and get ready for change because Your Promotion Is In Motion."

Pastor Paula White-Cain,
Senior Pastor, New Destiny Christian Center

"My good friend Greg Mauro has heard from heaven!

Your Promotion Is In Motion is a breakthrough word from God that will upgrade you into your new season of favor and divine destiny.

Isaiah 51:2 says, "When God called Abraham he was just one man...but when He blessed him, he became a GREAT nation..."

Now is your time for greatness! I believe that God will use *Your Promotion Is In Motion* to shift you into His mighty promotion for your life, your family, your ministry and your future!"

Rev. Samuel Rodriguez,
President, National Hispanic Christian Leadership Conf.

"In Greg Mauro's book, *Your Promotion Is In Motion*, there are seven chapters that are page after page of important, revelatory nuggets, that when applied to your daily life and walk will progress you from one level to another in God's assignment for you."

Perry Stone,
Founder and President, Voice of Evangelism

"Every Leader Must Read This Book!   Greg Understands Ministry As Few People Do."

Dr. Mike Murdock,
Senior Pastor, The Wisdom Center

"If anybody has the authority to speak on the topic of *Your Promotion Is In Motion* it is Greg Mauro.

He has faithfully served God's prophet Dr. Morris Cerullo for over three decades and has seen this ministry flourish into the global phenomenon that it is.

Greg is an incredible leader, armor bearer, worship leader, father, and friend.

I could not recommend this book more highly. These seven principles will take your life to the next level."

Jurgen Matthesius,
Lead Pastor, C3 San Diego"

"Oftentimes the road to promotion is paved with more transition than we're comfortable discussing. My friend, Greg Mauro, bravely speaks prophetically and brilliantly to God's process of promotion by leading readers through the journey from obscurity to destiny. Written from the lens of a genuine servant's heart, *Your Promotion Is In Motion: Seven Words From God That Will Promote You To Your Greater Destiny*" reminds every Christian to remember the words of the One whose promotion is irrevocable, undeniable, and irrefutable."

Sergio De La Mora,
Author, Paradox and Lead Pastor of Cornerstone
Church of San Diego

"*Your Promotion Is In Motion* written by my dear friend Rev. Greg Mauro contains lots of spiritual nuggets. The importance of this book from the stable of one that has put in over three decades serving under his mentor, at a time like this when people are very impatient serving others, cannot be over emphasized.

The character behind a tested dream is a life of inspiration, and spiritual power. As you read these words, you will step into God's end-time destiny, because your promotion is indeed in motion! God is in the business of preparing men and women to impact their generations far beyond their abilities.

I hereby endorse and recommend this unique book to every Christian and indeed every Minister of the gospel who wants to be relevant in Gods end-time agenda."

Pastor Ayo Oritsejafor, (OFR)
Founder and Senior Pastor, Word of Life Bible Church,
Warri, Nigeria

"Greg Mauro is not only my brother, but has served as a trusted advisor to our church leadership for over 30 years. *Your Promotion Is In Motion* will not only inspire pastors and church leaders, but also a generation of families and congregations seeking to live up to their full,

God-given potential. It is like a spiritual shot of adrenaline straight from heaven!"

Gary Mauro,
Founding Pastor, Calvary Chapel Sawgrass,
The Local Church

"Greg Mauro has devoted himself to building the Kingdom! *Your Promotion Is In Motion* has been lived out through Greg's life first hand. This book is a great encouragement to hold on to God's Promises through the valleys of life as well as the mountaintops. Greg is an anointed leader and everyone who applies the principles of this book will be greatly blessed."

Matthew Barnett,
New York Times Best Selling Author,
Co-Founder of The Dream Center

"Greg Mauro has faithfully stood by the side of one of the greatest men of God that has ever lived on this planet. *Your Promotion Is In Motion* is a word from God that will upgrade you to your new season of favor.

These powerful seven game-changing words that God gave to Greg will be the keys that will promote you and your dreams to the next level!"

Steve Munsey,
Senior Pastor, Family Christian Center

"Greg has served Dr. Morris & Theresa Cerullo faithfully and with a spirit of excellence for 32 years. This book written by such a legend is well overdue. This 6 foot 9 inch man is not only a giant in stature but also a giant in the Body of Christ. I honor you sir, and I believe whole-heartedly that the baton has been deservedly passed on, so run with it - Legacy!

Your Promotion Is In Motion will take you step by step to show you that God has a greater plan for your life, revealing how to overcome the challenges you may be facing. You may find yourself identifying with certain chapters as the words and scriptures expressed prick your heart. This is a good thing. That means God is speaking directly to you! I have always preached that 'pro' means 'before'. 'Motion' means 'movement'. You cannot be in a motion if you are not moving! It is impossible - We all want promotion but it cannot be achieved by being stagnant.

This book will take you out of a place of complacency, your comfort zone and take you to a place of illumination and a revelation of who you are. Your movement towards promotion will be activated, manifested and your spirit will be ignited. You literally won't be able to stop reading this book! Enjoy and remember YOUR PROMOTION IS IN MOTION!"

Bishop John Francis
Senior Pastor, Ruach City Church, UK

TABLE OF CONTENTS

FOREWORD

It has been one of the great joys of our lives for Theresa and me to watch the anointing of God increase upon Greg's life these past three decades.

Greg has become more than a blessing – he is a dear, spiritual son and an extension of my ministry. His life has demonstrated the message in the pages of, "Your Promotion Is In Motion".

Those that come under the special anointing imparted in this book will truly become an extension of the blessing and power that awaits those who will decide to feed their future and not their fears and step into their greater destiny.

I will never forget sending Greg to live in England with his young family as my European Director for nearly seven years. Together we saw Great Britain shaken as 16,000+ a night jammed the historic Earl's Court Auditorium for annual week-long Mission To London Meetings, 50,000+ packed the Olympic Stadium for over 3 nights in Moscow,

Russia, just months after the Iron Curtain came down, together, we pioneered Christian television across Europe, and so much more...

Over the years, Greg has served as my Crusade Director, Television Co-Host, Writer, Accountant, Media Buyer, Marketing and Public Relations Man, Emcee of my conferences, and most of all, my Associate Minister.

Every Pastor - leader - believer that wants God to use their life in a greater way – will be deeply blessed – enriched - and challenged - by the encouraging words of this book.

God's Servant,

Morris Cerullo
President, Morris Cerullo World Evangelism
Legacy International Center

INTRODUCTION

I am a man in transition. Whether you know it or not, so are you...

"Your Promotion Is In Motion" is the result of seven specific, personal, life-changing words of challenge, empowerment and encouragement that God dramatically spoke to me in my own season of transition.

I didn't find them on You Tube or search for them on Google, but they came directly from the presence of God, from His word to a heart of desperation.

I was not looking to write this book, this is a message that looked for me and continues to write me.

The process of giving birth to God's greater destiny for your life – transition – will be painful, but necessary and mostly, rewarding. (Any woman that has given birth will

3

no doubt say amen!) God directed me to share these seven words with you. They will elevate, upgrade and deliver you to your greater destiny and reward...

In a scripture that has become the voice of God over my transition, Isaiah 51:2 (NLT) says, *"Think about Abraham your ancestor and Sarah who gave birth to your nation. Abraham was ONLY ONE MAN when I called him, but when I blessed him HE BECAME A GREAT NATION."*

I believe you are reading this because now is your time for God to increase your kingdom influence, and like Abraham, take you from being only one man to stepping into God's blessing for something much greater. This is a word from God that will take you there.

Internationally respected leadership expert, John Maxwell said, "Success is when you add value to yourself. Significance is when you add value to others. Grow beyond yourself. By improving yourself, the world is

4

made better. <u>We cannot achieve our wildest dreams by remaining who we are</u>."

You and I were chosen by God for much more than to count our blessings and attain personal success. You and I were born to live a life of impact, significance, giving, legacy and to BE a blessing. Christianity never was intended to be a consumer-driven spectator sport!

In some sobering words that challenge the culture of the day we live in, Rusty Rustenbach recently said, "You and I live in an age when only a rare minority of individuals desire to spend their lives in pursuit of objectives which are bigger than they are. <u>In our age, for most people, when they die, it will be as though they never lived</u>"

You are reading this book because you are not like most people. God has marked your life for much more than you have ever imagined.

Psalms 105:19 (NLT) says, *"Until the __time__ came to fulfill his dreams, the Lord __tested__ Joseph's character"*.

Every dream has a time and every dream has a test. You have been through the test, and now is your time to step into God's big dream for your life. And there is no doubt, and there will be no delay... Your Promotion Is In Motion!

"Think about Abraham

your ancestor and Sarah

who gave birth to your nation.

Abraham was ONLY ONE MAN

when I called him,

but when I blessed him

HE BECAME A

GREAT NATION"

Isaiah 51:2 (NLT)

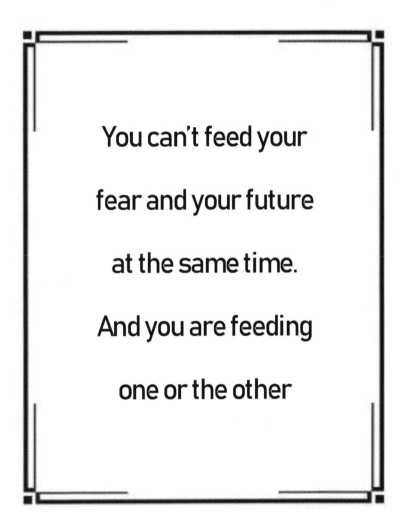

You can't feed your

fear and your future

at the same time.

And you are feeding

one or the other

CHAPTER
ONE

STOP HIDING FROM YOUR PROMOTION

"But when they looked for Saul, he had disappeared! So they asked the Lord, "Where is he?" and the Lord replied, "He is hiding among the baggage..."
(1 Samuel 10:22-23 NLT)

You can't feed your fears and your future at the same time. And you are feeding one or the other...

God sees something greater <u>in you</u> than you see in yourself.

And, God sees something greater <u>for your life</u> – your family – your finances – your ministry – your future –your influence - than you see for yourself...

Every great man – every great woman - that has been called by God – has dealt with fear. The message of this book is that you and I serve a great God who will find you in your hiding place of reluctance, insecurity and fear – meet you there – encourage you there – remind you who you are and who He is - and bring you out!

God met Gideon in his hiding place.

"Now the Angel of the Lord came and sat under the terebinth tree which was in Ophrah, which belonged to Joash, the Abiezrite, while his son Gideon threshed wheat in the winepress, in order to hide it from the Midianites. <u>And the Angel of the Lord appeared to him, and said to him, "The Lord is with you, you mighty man of valor!</u>" (Judges 6:11-12 NKJV)

God saw something in Gideon that Gideon did not see in himself.

God saw something in Gideon that his own father did not see in him. Even at your lowest point, God sees something greater in you and for you than you or anybody else sees.

God doesn't see what you are; He sees what you can be…

This powerful truth began to change my life 32 years ago in an Oral Roberts University student chapel service when our guest speaker, Dr. Morris Cerullo powerfully ministered from his classic, "Proof Producers" message.

He shared how in one verse of the 16th chapter of the Gospel of Mark, Jesus rebuked all eleven disciples for not believing those who said He was resurrected…but then in the very next verse He turned to these fearful, running from the cross, Jesus-denying, unbelieving disciples, encouraged them and entrusted them with the Great Commission:

Check it out…

Afterward He appeared unto the eleven as they sat at meat, and <u>upbraided them with their unbelief and hardness of heart</u>, because they believed not them, which had seen him after he was risen. (Mark 16:14 KJV)

Then in Jesus' next breath, He turns to this same group and instead of sending them back to square one, or giving up on them, or delaying their destiny, He commissions them!

And he said unto them, <u>Go ye into all the world, and preach the gospel to every creature</u>. (Mark 16:15 KJV)

WOW! In a simple, but profound and powerful statement, Morris explained how God could entrust and empower these men in their weakness, and how He still does the same with you and me, when he said...

"<u>GOD IS NOT DEPENDING ON ANYTHING YOU POSSESS; GOD IS DEPENDING ON WHAT HE CAN MAKE OF YOU</u>!"
(MORRIS CERULLO)

I wrote this book to tell you that I discovered the greatest faith in all the world is not the faith you have in God, but <u>the greatest faith in all the world is the faith that God has in you</u>!

God met Moses in his hiding place - in his fear and rejection- in the backside of the desert. He met Moses not to rebuke him or to embarrass him but to encourage him right where he was, and to bring him out!

We read in Exodus why Moses, a Hebrew, who was raised in the Egyptian palace of the Pharaoh, found himself hiding from his destiny in the backside of the desert.

"Many years later, when Moses had grown up, he went out to visit his own people, the Hebrews, and he saw how hard they were forced to work. During his visit, he saw an Egyptian beating one of his fellow Hebrews. After looking in all directions to make sure no one was watching, Moses killed the Egyptian and hid the body in the sand. The next day, when Moses went out to visit his

people again, he saw two Hebrew men fighting. "Why are you beating up your friend?" Moses said to the one who had started the fight. The man replied, "Who appointed you to be our prince and judge? Are you going to kill me as you killed the Egyptian yesterday?" Then Moses was afraid, thinking, "Everyone knows what I did." And sure enough, Pharaoh heard what had happened and he tried to kill Moses. But Moses fled from Pharaoh and went to live in the land of Midian." (Exodus 2:11-15 NLT)

All of a sudden, Moses became a man without a country. He went from having everything to having nothing. A great man with a great calling in a place of great fear, rejection and hiding.

There were three 40-year stages to Moses' life:

The First 40 years, Moses thought he was a somebody.
The Second 40 years, he found out he was a nobody.

Then in his Final 40 years, Moses learned what God could do with a somebody who knew he was a nobody!

God met Moses in his place of fear, hiding and rejection to encourage him and to bring him out into his promotion. It was God's time to show Himself strong on Moses' behalf, to bring him out and to fulfill his dreams by a demonstration of His power...

Even while Moses was hiding, his promotion was in motion... and so is yours!

You are not reading this book by accident. Now is God's time to visit you, remind you who you are, who He is, and for you to stop feeding your fear and start feeding your future! This is your personal, defining moment.

At Moses' defining moment, God supernaturally met him in the backside of the desert of Midian and spoke out of a burning bush, *"Look! The cry of the people of Israel has*

reached Me, *(your promotion is not only about you, but mostly about how God wants to use you to impact the people He is sending you to)* **and I have seen how harshly the Egyptians abuse them. Now go, for I am sending you to Pharaoh. You must lead my people Israel out of Egypt." (Exodus 3:9-10 NLT)**

This book is your burning bush, may God speak to you from every page!

For every fear – every insecurity – every weakness – that Moses struggled with and verbalized– God did not rebuke him - or chastise him – He reassured him and equipped him!

When Moses doubted himself and asked the same question many great men and women have asked, "Who am I (to appear before Pharaoh)?" God answered, "I will be with you."

When you struggle with who you are and wonder how you can accomplish God's great destiny for your life, the

Lord will remind you that <u>He is with YOU</u>!

David said, "I will fear no evil <u>for You are with me</u>..."
(Psalm 23:4 NKJV)

When Moses asked, "Who will I say sent me?" God gave him a great weapon, His name, Yahweh!

Just like Moses, God is not sending you out in your own name, or in your own ability. He is sending you out in the Name that is above every name, Jesus Christ, the Son of the Living God, who said, *"You didn't choose Me. I chose you. I appointed you to go and produce lasting fruit, so that <u>the Father will give you whatever you ask for, using my Name</u>!" (John 15:16 NLT)*

I am convinced that whatever you or I ask the Father in the Name of Jesus to help equip us to fulfill God's great, appointed destiny for our life and produce lasting fruit, He will give it to you!

When Moses doubted himself saying, "What if they don't believe me or listen to me?" The Lord gave Moses His miracle-working power...

When Moses reluctantly continued, **"I'm not very good with words. I never have been, and I'm not now, even though you have spoken to me, I get tongue-tied and my words get tangled**.*" (Exodus 4:10 NLT)*

The Lord told Moses, *"Now go! I will be with you as you speak, and I will instruct you in what to say."*
(Exodus 4: 12 NLT)

Yet, even after receiving all this encouragement from the Lord, Moses was still not quite convinced, so God met him again at his place of doubt and reluctance. He didn't reprove him, but instead gave him even more help and encouragement in the person of his brother Aaron, who God sent to be Moses' assistant.

<u>GOD IS NOT LOOKING FOR WAYS TO SHORT CIRCUIT YOUR DESTINY</u>. <u>GOD IS LOOKING FOR WAYS TO HELP YOU FULFILL YOUR DESTINY</u>!

The God you serve is a patient God that is 100% invested in showing Himself strong on your behalf and giving you everything you need to successfully fulfill your destiny!

Thirty-two years ago through a dramatic, divine encounter, God stopped me in my tracks and called me to serve and stand by the side of the ministry of Dr. Morris Cerullo. I share the story in my book, *The Blessing of Serving Another Man's Ministry*. For the past three plus decades, serving as Dr. Cerullo's Vice President of Ministries has been the privilege and experience of a lifetime.

As a result, God has singularly blessed my life – my family – and my ministry serving Morris and Theresa these past

30+ years. By God's grace, I have been faithful. My wife and family have been faithful.

My motive has been to serve – to be a blessing – without ulterior or hidden agendas.

Many times, world-renowned Pastor Tommy Barnett has very graciously referred to me as "America's number one number two man!"

I have been blessed. I have been beyond fulfilled. God has given me success. I love Morris and Theresa and what God has privileged us to experience and accomplish together for the glory of God and His kingdom.

But I discovered that while God can use you – even in your success you can become comfortable and hide from your greater destiny...

Everybody likes to be comfortable and successful, but I wrote this book from a painful discovery: <u>your greater future destiny can die in your present comfort zone of success</u>!

Like the mother eagle – who begins to remove some of the comfortable things from the nest, the soft twigs, the leaves, and the thatch so that her baby eaglets begin to realize it's time to move from the comfort of their nest – to spread their own wings and fly – for some time – Dr. Cerullo and the Lord have been nudging and prodding this 6'9" eagle to begin to spread his wings in a greater way...

One of the most unusual stories in the Bible is found in 1 Samuel 10:20-24 (NLT). Maybe you can relate to it. I know I did. Let me explain...

"So, Samuel brought all the tribes of Israel before the Lord... but when they looked for Saul, he had disappeared! So they asked the Lord, "Where is he?" And the Lord replied, "<u>HE IS HIDING AMONG THE BAGGAGE.</u>"

So they found him and brought him out... Then Samuel said to all the people, "This is the man the Lord has chosen as your king. No one in all Israel is like him!" And all the people shouted, "Long live the king!"

WHEN IT WAS TIME FOR SAUL TO STEP INTO HIS PROMOTION AND BE PRESENTED AS ISRAEL'S KING, SAUL DISAPPEARED AND WAS HIDING!

When Samuel found Saul hiding behind the baggage, he graciously brought him out, gave him a grand and glorious introduction to all of Israel, never speaking a word publicly about Saul's behind the scenes fearfulness and reluctance. God did not embarrass him, or change His mind, or delay Saul's destiny, instead He celebrated Saul and promoted him!

Neither will God forsake you or embarrass you when He finds you in your hiding place. Instead, He will encourage you, remind you who you are, who He is, empower you, bring you out, back you up and promote you!

Maybe you can relate. Maybe you know that there is more for you. I want to encourage you. Now is your time to come out of hiding from behind the baggage of your fears, your weakness, your failures, your excuses and even your successes, and take the next step into your greater destiny.

God knows where you are and will encourage you even now in your hiding place. He will meet you there, remind you who you are, and who He is, and bring you out!

And you are in good company...
God met Gideon in his hiding place...
He met Moses in his hiding place...
He met Jonah in his hiding place...
He met Adam in his hiding place...
And He met Saul in his hiding place...

As Saul came out from hiding behind the baggage, God announced: *"This is the man the Lord has chosen as your king. No one in all Israel is like him!" And all the people shouted, "Long live the king!" (1 Samuel 10:24 NLT)*

Today God is making a grand announcement over you: "You are the man - you are the woman – that the Lord has chosen for a greater purpose... there is no one in all the world like you! The people that need you – those that I have called you to help – they are looking for you, they are waiting for you. Listen to them shouting now as you rise up to step into your destiny, "Long live _____ (insert your name). There is no one in the Kingdom of God like you!"

Your destiny is too great and your life is too short to play it safe in your relationship with God and His great promotion for your life. God loves risk-takers...

Faith always takes a risk...

No risk, no reward...

And know this: The greatest battle over your life is what you believe about God and what you believe He believes about you.

There are two voices over your promotion...the voice of the accuser – and the voice of the Intercessor.

There were two voices over Peter's life as the baton was about to be passed to him from Jesus when it was Peter's time to step into his promotion...

"And the Lord said, "Simon, Simon! Indeed Satan has asked for you, that he may sift you as wheat. But I have prayed for you, that your faith should not fail; and when you have returned to Me, strengthen your brethren" *(Luke 22:31-32 NKJV)*

Though Satan will try to sift you, know this: Jesus is praying for you! And the voice of the Intercessor is much greater in heaven and in earth than the voice of the accuser!

I discovered that in my season of promotion (and every day of my life), the greatest investment you can make in your life is spending time in God's Word and establishing the voice of God as the greatest voice in your life.

You will be prepared, encouraged and propelled into your promotion by the transforming of your mind through daily meditating on God's Word, prayer and associating with those that challenge you to grow and reach your dreams.

When it was Joshua's time to step into his promotion, God told him, *"**Study this book of instruction continually. Meditate in it day and night...Only then will you prosper and succeed in all you do**.*"*(Joshua 1:8 NLT)*

Listen to this prophetic declaration from Morris Cerullo that has encouraged and challenged me and many others countless times through the years...it is a word from God for you wherever you are right now...

"YOU ARE NOT WHAT THE DEVIL SAYS YOU ARE, BUT YOU ARE WHAT GOD SAYS YOU ARE, AND TODAY YOU ARE STEPPING INTO YOUR END-TIME DESTINY."

Why don't you say it: "I am not what the devil says I am. I am what God says I am. And today, I am stepping in to my end time destiny!"

With all my heart, I believe that now is your time to hear the word of the Lord encourage you, and take you by the hand to bring you out of your hiding place - and for you to take the next step into your greater destiny.

Your promotion, and more importantly, those that the Lord has destined for you to impact, are waiting for you!

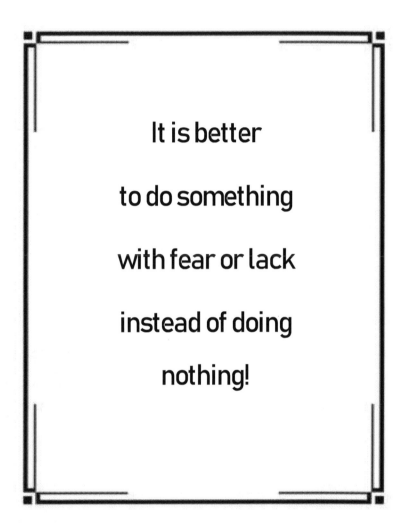

It is better

to do something

with fear or lack

instead of doing

nothing!

CHAPTER
TWO

THINKING LITTLE OF YOURSELF IS NOT A VIRTUE

"...<u>Although you may think little of yourself, are you not the leader of the Tribes of Israel</u>?" (1 Samuel 15:17 NLT)

Five chapters after Saul was found hiding from his promotion, the prophet Samuel revealed the character flaw that ultimately cost Saul his destiny...

"Then Samuel said to Saul, "Stop! Listen to what the Lord told me last night!" "What did he tell you?" Saul asked. And Samuel told him, "<u>ALTHOUGH YOU MAY THINK LITTLE OF YOURSELF, are you not the leader of the tribes of Israel? The Lord has anointed you king of Israel</u>... So because you have rejected the command of the Lord, he has rejected you as king." (1 Samuel 15:16-23 NLT)

29

Saul was a giant on the outside, but thought much less of himself on the inside...

Thinking little of yourself is not a virtue. It is not healthy humility. It is a demonic destiny-destroying lie that if left unchecked feeds fear and <u>unbelief!</u>

Proverbs 23:7 NKJV says, ***"For as he thinks in his heart, so is he..."***

How you see yourself is how others will also see you.

Insecurity, thinking little of yourself, is what caused the ten spies and the nation of Israel to miss their destiny, ***"<u>We were in our own sight as grasshoppers</u>, and so we were in their sight." (Numbers 13:33 KJV)***

It is what caused the one-talented servant to hide his talent in the earth.

"Then the servant with the one bag of silver came and said, "Master I knew you were a harsh man, harvesting crops you didn't plant and gathering crops you didn't cultivate. I was afraid I would lose your money so I hid it in the earth. Here is your money back." But the master replied, "You wicked and lazy servant!" (Matthew 25:24-26 NLT)

No doubt the one-talented servant compared himself unfavorably to the other "higher talented" servants that were entrusted with five talents and two talents, as the Bible records all three received their talents at the same time and place.

Comparison is a trap.

Comparison is a destiny-destroyer.

When we compare, we either think less of ourselves than we should or more of ourselves than we should.

The one talented servant thought less of himself...

Regarding comparison, Stewart B. Johnson said, "Our business in life is not to get ahead of others, but to get ahead of ourselves, to break our own records, to outstrip our yesterday by today, to do our work with more force than ever before!"

The one-talented servant thought little of himself because he fell into the trap of comparing himself to others that seemed to have more.

He then revealed that he saw God through the lens of his inferiority and fear when he said, **"Master, I knew you were a harsh man."** (Matthew 25:24 NLT)

My dear friend and great men's ministry pioneer, Edwin Louis Cole always said, "What you believe about God will either attract you to Him or repel you from Him."

The one-talented servant's life was a do-nothing life that was frozen by fear, inferiority and the lie that God is a harsh God...

Because he thought little of himself, and because he saw God as a harsh God, he gave in to fear and laziness, stalled in his comfort zone and did nothing.

To step into your season of promotion, you must move. Put feet to your faith! Your promotion can only be in motion when YOU are in motion toward it!

Action changes feelings...

Inaction reinforces negative feelings...

<u>IT IS BETTER TO **DO SOMETHING** WITH FEAR OR LACK INSTEAD OF DOING NOTHING!</u>

Like the loaves and fishes, God can take what you think is your little and bless it and multiply it to make it more than enough to fulfill His greater destiny for your life when you put even what little you think you have into His great hands.

God's power, supernatural provision, divine intervention and spiritual breakthrough come <u>when you do something</u>! That is what happened when the four lepers, who were SITTING just a few feet from their miracle, at the entrance of the gates of Samaria, decided to MAKE A MOVE...

"<u>Why should we sit here waiting to die</u>? We will starve if we stay here, but with the famine in the city, we will starve if we go back there. <u>So we might as well go</u> out and surrender to the Aramean army. If they let us live, so much the better. But if they kill us, we would have died anyway. <u>So at twilight they set out for the camp of the Arameans</u>. But <u>when they came to the edge of the camp, no one was there!</u> For <u>the Lord had caused the Aramean army to hear the clatter of speeding chariots and the galloping of horses and the sound of a great</u>

army approaching...when the men with leprosy arrived at the edge of the camp, they went into one tent after another, eating and drinking wine; and they carried off silver and gold and clothing..." (2 Kings 7:3-8 NLT)

These four lepers may have been the weakest - most improbable people for God to use in the entire nation of Israel. They had nothing to give to God, but they decided to feed their future and not their fear – and God used these unlikely four lepers as His instruments to bring incredible blessing and promotion, not just to themselves – but also to the entire nation of Israel!

Here is a game changing truth I discovered: God promises to turn your weakness into strength, under one condition...

Hebrews 11:34 NLT says, "God will turn your weakness into strength and will make you strong IN THE BATTLE."

He will not make you strong on the sidelines! He will make

you strong <u>IN the battle</u>, when you get back in the game and begin to make a move toward the greater thing that He has called you to do...

If you will use what God has given you – and take a step toward the greater thing God has called you to do – he will turn your weakness into strength – make you strong – and give you more!

Why don't you declare this again: ***"I am not what the devil says I am. I am what God says I am. And today, I am stepping in to my end-time destiny!"***

Your Master is not harsh...

He is full of praise and encouragement – and will even take the little you think you have and multiply it many fold, if you will just begin to use what God has given you. ***"Master, you gave me five bags of silver <u>to invest</u>, and I have earned five more. <u>The master was full of praise</u>.***

36

Well done, my good and faithful servant. You have been faithful in handling this small amount, <u>so now I will give you many more</u> responsibilities. <u>Let's celebrate together!</u>" (Matthew 25:20b-21 NLT)

The five-talented servant – and the two-talented servant – understood that what they had been given was not for them to keep – or to bury - but to give to somebody else - to invest! They valued what the Master had given them and why the Master gave it to them...

Don't hide what God has given you. Don't think little of what God has given you. <u>Somebody needs what you have. Somebody needs your words of encouragement. Somebody needs your prayers. Somebody needs the gift of God in your life.</u>

Many times since that day in 1987, I have remembered that great truth Morris Cerullo spoke at the ORU chapel,

*"**Jesus is not depending on anything that I possess, He is depending on one thing – <u>what He can make of me</u>!"***

Thirty plus years later, over and over again, God has proven this word true in my life and in the lives of countless others.

Without fear of contradiction, I boldly declare to you, "<u>God is not depending on anything that you possess – God is depending on one thing – what He can make of you</u>!"

Remember, because ***"<u>We are His workmanship,</u> created in Christ Jesus unto good works, which God hath before ordained that we should walk in them." (Ephesians 2:10 KJV),*** thinking little of yourself not a virtue, it is really thinking little of God and His workmanship in your life.

Why not decide to see God as He really is and see yourself as God sees you, because you are His great workmanship, and your promotion is in motion!

God doesn't see

what you are;

He sees

what you can be!

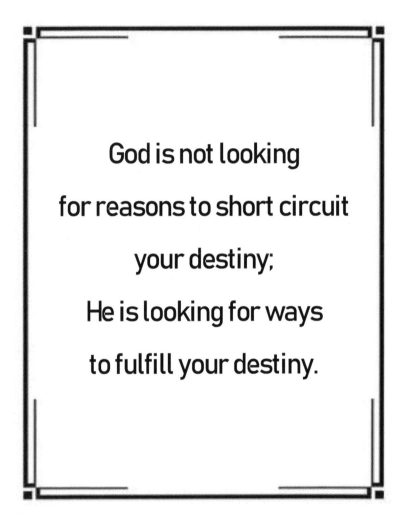

God is not looking

for reasons to short circuit

your destiny;

He is looking for ways

to fulfill your destiny.

CHAPTER
THREE

**YOUR MISTAKES DO NOT DISQUALIFY YOU FOR
WHAT GOD HAS QUALIFIED YOU FOR!**

*"So Abraham said to God, "May Ishmael live under your
special blessing!" As for Ishmael, I will bless him also,
just as you have asked." (Genesis 17:18, 20 NLT)*

I remember the cold conference room table nearly 30
years ago in Birmingham, England. It was my first ever-
citywide pastors meeting representing Dr. Cerullo with
about 50 conservative British pastors, inviting them to
join their hearts and hands together with Dr. Cerullo and
our Morris Cerullo World Evangelism team in a great
outreach for souls in their city.

I was so excited! The opportunity to talk with these great
leaders about the heartbeat of God – souls – and the

opportunity for us to partner together in prayer to reach the lost of their city would surely be something they were excited about too...

I soon realized these pastors were not as excited as I thought! The perceived cultural differences - suspicions – differences in style of ministry... If looks could kill, I would be in heaven right now and you would not be reading this book!

Right then and there, I whispered a prayer to God – put aside my prepared notes – looked these spiritual leaders in the eyes – and these were the words that came out of my mouth:

"How many around this table would like to know how you will never make a mistake in your ministry?"

I thought to myself, "Where did that come from? And what will I say next?!"

Then these were the words that came out of my mouth:

"Do you want to know how you will never make a mistake in your ministry?" I repeated. "I will tell you how you will never make a mistake in your ministry. <u>Just do nothing for God and you will never make a mistake in your ministry!</u>"

I told them that whatever differences they might have with Dr. Cerullo's style of ministry, one thing I could assure them, this was a man that lived his life for God and for the kingdom at one speed – and one speed only – Full speed!

I then outlined with these leaders the incredible sacrifices that Morris, Theresa, and their family have made these many decades to take the gospel to the nations of the world – because of his incredible passion for souls. I explained that if in the process of whole-heartedly going after the Great Commission – they felt they would have done things differently – God bless them – but one thing I could tell them is that when Morris Cerullo stands before God, he would not be reproved for not giving his all for King and kingdom!

The spirit in the room changed – the guarded looks softened – we put aside our differences in approach – joined our hearts and hands together for the sake of souls – and saw a great move of God in their city during the Morris Cerullo Birmingham Crusade, praise the Lord!

What am I saying? I am telling you this. Moses made mistakes – Abraham made mistakes – David made mistakes – Peter made mistakes - you and I will make mistakes...

But, as you step into your promotion, God will remind you that your mistakes have not disqualified you for what He alone has qualified and called you to!

Did you ever put your wife's life in danger to save yourself? Abraham did...

"Abraham introduced his wife Sarah by saying, "She is my sister." So King Abimelech of Gerar sent for Sarah and had her brought to him at his palace." (Genesis 20:2 NLT)

Abraham lied to King Abimelech. The father of our faith operated in fear and self-preservation, lying and handing over his beautiful wife, Sarah (who was destined to be mother to the nation of God's people), to Abimelech, so that the king would not kill Abraham and take his wife for himself!

A flawed betrayal to the two most important covenant relationships in Abraham's life – his covenant with God and his covenant with his wife...

Talk about a major mistake in his ministry! Abraham gave his wife to the heathen King Abimelech. The Bible says, *"But that night, <u>God came to Abimelech</u> in a dream and told him, "You are a dead man, for that woman you have taken is already married... now return the woman to her*

husband and he will pray for you, <u>for he is a prophet</u>!"
(Genesis 20:3, 7a NLT)

If I were God, I would have come to Abraham and told him, "<u>YOU</u> are a dead man!" But God defended guilty Abraham and instead confronted innocent King Abimelech!

Even in Abraham's weakness and compromise, God had his back! God would not let Abraham destroy his destiny. God did what Abraham should have done – and went in to the palace of King Abimelech and demanded that he return Sarah to her husband.

Not only did God fix Abraham's mistake, He corrected, honored and encouraged Abraham in the process!

Before the king that Abraham deceived, God called Abraham His prophet. God instructed the king to not only return Sarah to Abraham, but to humble himself and ask Abraham to pray for him!

Even in your mistakes and in your failures, God is not interested in embarrassing you or demoting you. Even at your weakest – at your lowest – I declare God's promotion for your life is still in motion!

God has not changed his mind concerning His great plan for your life. The Bible says, *"**For God's gifts and His call can never be withdrawn**." (Romans 11:29 NLT)*

God is not looking for reasons to short circuit your destiny; he is looking for ways to fulfill your destiny.

The Bible says God devises ways to bring us back to His presence – to bring us back to His purpose – even when we have been separated from Him and from His purpose.

My favorite scripture in the entire Word of God is 2 Samuel 14:14 NLT: *"All of us must die eventually. Our lives are like water spilled out on the ground, which cannot be gathered up again. **But God does not just*** *sweep life away; instead, He devises ways to bring us back when we have been separated from Him."*

Not only will God forgive you and turn your mistakes around, but when you are chosen by God, He will even bless your mistakes and cause them to serve your destiny!

Abraham asked God to bless his greatest mistake, Ishmael, and to even use Ishmael to fulfill great destiny. God said He would!

"So Abraham said to God, "May Ishmael live under your special blessing!" As for Ishmael, I will bless him also, just as you have asked. I will make him extremely fruitful and multiply his descendants. He will become the father of twelve princes, and I will make him a great nation." (Genesis 17:18, 20 NLT)

You know the story. Moses spent 40 years in the wilderness after he emotionally rose up in his own strength and killed the Egyptian that was oppressing his Hebrew brother.

Moses quickly discovered he had then become a man without a country. Egypt rejected him. Israel rejected him. But the mistake that drove Moses to the wilderness could not disqualify him for what God alone would qualify and call him to. His time in the wilderness was not wasted. Moses was humbled and God met him there.

The man that God would use to bring Israel out of Egypt was having Egypt taken out of him. God manifested himself to Moses in the wilderness.

Your time in the wilderness has not been wasted.
God will not allow your mistakes to define you; He will back you up, restore you, and use your mistakes to refine you.

He will even bless your mistakes and use them to work together for your good to get you to your destiny... (Romans 8:28)

Like Abraham – David – Peter – Moses -- and every other great man or woman that God has ever used – your setback is really God's set up for your comeback and your comeback begins today!
Your mistake has not disqualified you for what God has qualified you for!

I declare you are who God says you are and your promotion is still in motion!

Your mistake has not

disqualified you

for what God

has qualified you for!

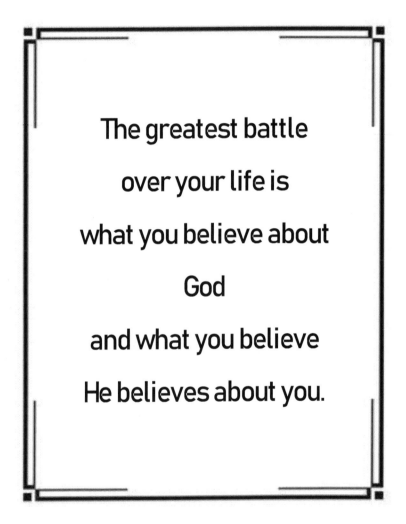

The greatest battle

over your life is

what you believe about

God

and what you believe

He believes about you.

CHAPTER FOUR

GOD WILL REMIND YOU THAT HE FOUND YOU

"I have found My servant David…" (Psalm 89:20 NLT)

One of our sons, Josh, played college football at Stanford University. In those days, Jim Harbaugh was the Head Coach. One of the first things Coach Harbaugh did when he became the football coach at Stanford was to have a huge 50-foot banner created that hung in clear view on the practice field everyday which said, "You either got better today…or got worse…you did not stay the same!"

And this truth is parallel in our relationship with God and His destiny for our life.

About the importance of growth, Gail Sheehy made a powerful statement, "No individual can measure his or her own impact. So what is one to do? Keep growing.

Do something every day to make yourself better able to give. Whatever talents, skills and resources you have, improve them to the point that people benefit from the overflow of your life. And keep giving. And let God worry about keeping score. If we don't change, we don't grow. If we don't grow, we are not really living. GROWTH DEMANDS A TEMPORARY SURRENDER OF SECURITY."

Christian author and leadership expert John Maxwell famously said, "We cannot achieve our wildest dreams by remaining who we are. Grow beyond yourself. By improving yourself, the world is made a better place."

What was true for Josh and his Stanford teammates is true for you and me. Each day is an opportunity to make a greater investment in our relationship with God and in our service to others. We are either growing or shrinking – but we do not remain the same.

I wrote this book out of God's gracious dealings with me

in my own season of transition. You are most likely reading this book because you are a person in transition.

Your promotion is in motion.

Promotion requires transition.

Transition is fueled by growth. And, as Gail Sheehy said, "Growth demands a temporary surrender of security."

Promotions die in the comfort zone.

For over three decades, I have been privileged to serve and be mentored by the life and ministry of Dr. Morris Cerullo. He has not only been a mentor, he has been an example. He has not only been an example, he has been a force of nature – a spiritual father - who has always pulled more out of me than I ever would have believed was inside - as we co-labored together in the ministry.

Every time we have sat together over the past three decades, I have always come away with a bigger challenge and a greater impartation of confidence and the anointing of God.

However, this time was different. It was greater. The stakes were higher. Morris and Theresa asked Jeri and I to come spend several days with them in San Diego to fellowship, pray and talk about future, to talk about Legacy. Morris let us know that it was time for us and others to step forward in a greater way. At age 87, it was time for the baton to be passed. It was time to step into God's greater destiny for our lives...

This would not be a small transition.

I left San Diego with a determination not to feed my fear – or my insecurity – or my comfort zone – but to feed my future.

I could not wait to get home and into the prayer closet.

It was there that God met me with the seven game changing words that imparted faith, supernatural strength and encouragement to me personally and that gave birth to the pages you are reading – including a powerful verse of scripture – a four-fold promise that brought His presence - His peace – His assurance – His strength...

God said if I would lay hold of these four truths that I am about to share in these remaining chapters – that I would experience the reality of what Dr. Cerullo spoke in that ORU chapel many years ago when he said, "God is not depending on what you possess. God is depending on what He can make of you!"

It is the incredible summary of God's dealing with David in Psalms that came alive to me as I heard God's voice say:

"I HAVE FOUND my servant David...I HAVE ANOINTED HIM with my holy oil... I WILL STEADY HIM with my hand...with My powerful arm, I WILL MAKE HIM STRONG." (Psalms 89:20-21 NLT)

Thirty words that summed up God's dealing with the eighth son of Jesse, the shepherd boy, David. These same words sum up God's dealing with you and me.

God exclaimed, "I HAVE found my servant David. I HAVE anointed him."

God celebrated what He gave birth to by reminding David and everyone else that would read these words, that it was He that initiated His relationship with David. He wanted to be sure that David remembered that it was God that found him and that it was God that anointed him, and not David, Samuel, Jesse or anyone else.

God boasted, "I have found my servant David! I have anointed him with my holy oil!"

Then God celebrated what He would do as David went forward into his great destiny: "I WILL steady him, I WILL make him strong" as He set into motion David's unlikely promotion.

Thirty words that had nothing to do with David – and everything to do with God...

Thirty words where God would take all the glory...

And David had nothing to do with it!

Like a proud father, God bragged, "I HAVE FOUND my servant, David..."

It is always good to remember who gave birth to the journey you and I are on. You are not a Christian because you chose God.

You are a child of God because He chose you. And you have a great destiny because God is a great God of purpose who has a great plan for your life!

*"**For I know he plans that I have for you**, not to harm you; plans to give you a hope and a future."*
(Jeremiah 29:11 NIV)

Jesus wanted to be sure His followers understood, "**You didn't choose me. I chose you. I appointed you to go and produce** lasting fruit, so that the Father will give you whatever you ask for using my name." (John 15:16 NLT)*

If you or I chose God, we could have made a mistake and not really had what it took to be a fruitful, proof-producing follower of Jesus Christ. But God doesn't make mistakes! Since it was God that chose you, and not you that chose Him, then God is the initiator and the One at work in you *"to will and to do of His good pleasure!"* *(Philippians 2:13 KJV)*

I want to congratulate you! You are now more than halfway through this message. I think it is a good time to take a little praise break to celebrate the God who found you, chose you and set into motion your promotion...

I like what Levi Lusko says, "<u>God didn't get stuck with you, He chose you</u>!"

God saw something in David that his own father did not see – something that the prophet Samuel did not see... God saw a king. And God sees greatness inside of you.

When Jesus looked at Simon...he saw a Peter.

When Jacob wrestled with God...God saw an Israel...

When God saw Abraham and Sarah childless, past the age of child bearing...He saw a great nation...

The greatest faith in all the word is the faith that God has in you!

God does not see what you are; He sees what you can be. God passed over David's seven older, more experienced, more qualified brothers to choose David.

The Bible says, when Samuel arrived at Jesse's house to anoint the next king of Israel, *"Samuel took one look at Jesse's eldest son, Eliab and thought, "Surely this is the Lord's anointed!"* **But the Lord said to Samuel, "Don't judge by his appearance or height,** *for I have rejected him."* **The Lord doesn't see things the way you see them. People judge by outward appearance, but the Lord looks at the heart."*

Then Jesse told his son Abinadab to step forward and walk in front of Samuel. But Samuel said, "This is not the one the Lord has chosen."

Next Jesse summoned Shimea, but Samuel said, "Neither is this the one the Lord has chosen." In the same way, all seven of Jesse's sons were presented to Samuel. But Samuel said to Jesse, "The Lord has not chosen any of these."

Then Samuel asked, "Are these all the sons you have?" "There is still the youngest," Jesse replied, "but he's out in the fields watching the sheep and goats."

"Send for him at once," Samuel said, "We will not sit down to eat until he arrives."

So Jesse sent for him. He was dark and handsome with beautiful eyes. And the Lord said, "THIS IS THE ONE, ANOINT HIM." (1 Samuel 16:6-12 NLT)

Today, listen to the proud voice of your God and your Father over your life as He points His mighty finger of destiny in your direction and says, "You are the one, receive My anointing!"

The foundation of your identity – the foundation of your destiny – the foundation of your confidence – is in knowing that you are chosen by God and that God who began a good work in you is faithful to complete it. God knows what He is doing!

He is not just the author – He is also the finisher...

"Looking unto Jesus, the author and finisher of our faith..." (Hebrews 12:2 KJV)

Sometimes God will speak to us at the most unexpected places. I will never forget this time. Recently I finished my workout at the gym dripping sweat, as I heard the unmistakable, firm and encouraging voice of God speak inside of me, **"Greg, I have made a great investment in your life, and I plan on getting a great return on my investment in you!**"

Wow...

Listen to this...

When a stockbroker has a stock that is plummeting and is experiencing a major setback, what many stockbrokers do is sell and cut their losses. That is what many people do with you and me when we fail or disappoint them in one way or another. But God said to me, "Greg, when My people begin to plummet, and when My people begin to fall and experience a setback, I don't sell. I buy more. I invest more in them!"

You see, God invests more in you when you are down so that He will get a greater return when you rise! Just like the stockbroker that buys the troubled stock at its low point –sees the great growth potential – and is rewarded when he invests and it rises, God too gets the glory and receives a greater return when he invests in you and your promotion even at what you and others may think is your low point.

God is still fully invested in you and your promotion!

God has made a great investment in your life. He is a patient investor. He will get a great return on His great investment in you!

At the moment He found you – and chose you –, He began a good work in you that He is faithful to see through to a great completion!

And God not only chose you and set your promotion in motion; He gave you divine capability to successfully fulfill your destiny... Now, He will remind you that He anointed you.

If you will put yourself

in a position to need

the anointing,

you will experience

the anointing.

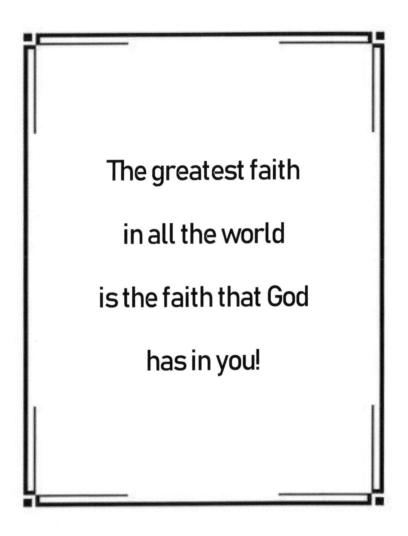

The greatest faith

in all the world

is the faith that God

has in you!

CHAPTER
FIVE

GOD WILL REMIND YOU THAT HE ANOINTED YOU!

I have anointed him with my holy oil... (Psalms 89:20)

God didn't just find you – then choose you – and then leave you on your own to fulfill His great purpose for your life - your family - your ministry – while He sits back, folds His arms, and says, "Now show Me what you've got!"

The God of the Old Testament was the God of "Show me what you've got!"

That lasted for all of ten minutes until Moses descended Mt Sinai with the 10 Commandments to discover Israel had already broken them all as he smashed the tablets in frustration and disappointment.

All along God had another plan...

The God of the New Testament is the God of "I've seen what you've got, <u>now let Me show you what I've got</u>!"

He is the God that chose to give birth to a new covenant – an "inside-out" relationship -- where He would take of His Spirit – His anointing – and put INSIDE of you and me, <u>the SAME Spirit</u> that raised Jesus from the dead! (Romans 8:11)

"Moreover, I will give you a new heart and put a new spirit WITHIN you, and I will remove the heart of stone from your flesh and give you a heart of flesh'" (Ezekiel 36:26 AMP)

God doesn't live in buildings. Now YOU and I are the temple of the Holy Spirit and Christ (the Anointed One), lives inside of you!

"To whom God would make known what is the riches of the glory of <u>this mystery</u> among the Gentiles, which is

Christin you, the hope of glory!" (Colossians 1:27 KJV)

The anointing is God's empowerment to fulfill His destiny for your life. The anointing of God is not an "it", but a Person. The word, *anoint* means, "to rub on or rub in". The anointing upon and within your life is nothing less than the person of God the Holy Spirit rubbing off on you!

When God finds you – chooses you – calls you – he also anoints you! David was anointed the moment he was chosen...

The Lord told his prophet Samuel to, "...**Go to the house of Jesse in Bethlehem, for I have selected one of his sons to be my king...**"

"And the Lord said, 'This is the one, anoint him!'

"So as David stood there among his brothers, _Samuel_

71

took the flask of olive oil he had brought and anointed David with the oil. And the Spirit of the Lord came powerfully upon David from that day on."
(1 Samuel 16:12-13 NLT)

When God calls you, immediately He anoints you. The Spirit of the Lord is powerfully upon you! Activating and operating under that anointing is another story...

David was anointed to be the king of Israel around the age of 15, though his promotion did not come until he was 30 years of age. He did not receive the anointing to be the king of Israel when he took the throne at 30 years of age. He had the anointing from the moment God chose him as a teenage boy. And so do you!

Every man – every woman – that God calls – that God anoints - goes through a process to get to their destiny...

Jacob went 20 years from God meeting him at Bethel

before he came back to Bethel for his name change Blessing encounter…

Joseph went 13 years from being left in the pit to being promoted to the palace…

Moses went 40 years from the isolation of the backside of the desert to the promotion encounter of the burning bush…

Abraham, 30 years from obeying God and leaving Haran to the birth of the promise, Isaac…

The anointing of God will keep you in the process and bring you to your place of destiny, increase and blessing…

Like every gift that God gives, <u>the anointing will only work and increase if you use it</u>. It is not for us to wear as a badge of honor, or to give us a title or a successful ministry. The anointing is God's holy presence upon you to empower you to minister to the needs of those that God has called you to!

If you will put yourself in a position to need the anointing, you will experience the anointing!

Jesus explained the purpose and the promise of the anointing, *"The Spirit of the Lord is upon Me BECAUSE He hath anointed me TO PREACH the gospel to the poor, He hath sent me TO HEAL the brokenhearted, To PREACH DELIVERANCE to the captives, and recovering of sight to the blind, TO SET AT LIBERTY them that are bruised, TO PREACH the acceptable year of the Lord!" (Luke 4:18-19 KJV)*

You and I will experience the anointing when we get out of our comfort zones and begin to do what the anointing upon us was given to us to enable us to do...

When we shift our focus from GETTING a blessing to BEING a blessing, God's anointing will empower you.

When we depend on God's anointing to minister to the needs of those that need a miracle, and when we DO SOMETHING like open our mouth to share the good news of Jesus Christ with someone that is lost, even when we are not sure what we are going to say – the anointing upon you will be activated...

I will never forget when I first came to work for Dr. Cerullo in San Diego in 1987. The only department that was hiring was the Accounting Department. Although my heart's desire was to help Dr. Cerullo in the Ministries Department, I knew the Lord had called me to serve MCWE, so I stepped through the door that the Lord had opened and started my ministry with MCWE as a Cost Accountant.

Many times God will give us an opportunity to show ourselves faithful in something that we may not want to do, so He can promote you to do what you really want to do.

I decided that my position at MCWE would not limit the vision God had put in my heart for souls. So, on Saturday mornings I would carry a cross around the city of San Diego and share the good news of Jesus Christ with anyone that would listen. It's hard to miss a 6'9" guy carrying a 10- foot cross!

Well, one Saturday, as I was walking with the cross, I came across a mysterious building covered with mirror tinted windows and no sign identifying the name or nature of the business that had hundreds of cars in the parking lot. I was curious...

I walked to the front door with my cross, opened the door, and was amazed at what I saw...a temporary casino had been set up inside this building with several hundred people sitting around scores of tables playing black jack, poker, etc.

The ceiling was a low eight-foot false ceiling, and lo and

behold standing before these hundreds of Saturday morning casino patrons is a nearly 7-foot man with a 10-foot cross!

To top it off, I immediately drew the attention of several large bouncers that were stationed at the back wall...

Talk about putting yourself in a position to need the anointing!

I knew that I had maybe 60 seconds before I would be shown the door. The bouncers were walking toward me. Every eye in the place was on the cross carrying giant that interrupted their Saturday morning card games – so I quickly prayed, and these were the words that God put in my mouth:

"How many here would like to know a hand that will never lose?" I heard myself ask...

Then I heard this answer, "It's the hand of Jesus and His hand is stretched out to you right now where you are! You can give your fears and your pain and your sins to Him right now by just raising your hand and putting it in His hand!"

The bouncers were now about 10 steps away... Hands went up across the room!!
I quickly said, "Let's pray!" and led this room full of unsuspecting Saturday morning card players in a prayer to receive the hand of Jesus into their lives from that day forward, just as the bouncers met me and kindly escorted me from the room, phew!

You will have the anointing when you do something that you need the anointing to do!

When you tell God you are ready to step into something bigger than yourself, His anointing will be there!

If you use what God has given you, He will give you more...

The former Arizona Cardinals Head Coach, Bruce Arians, always said, "No risk-it no biscuit!"

Faith always takes a risk for God, and the anointing will always be your enablement and reward when you do!

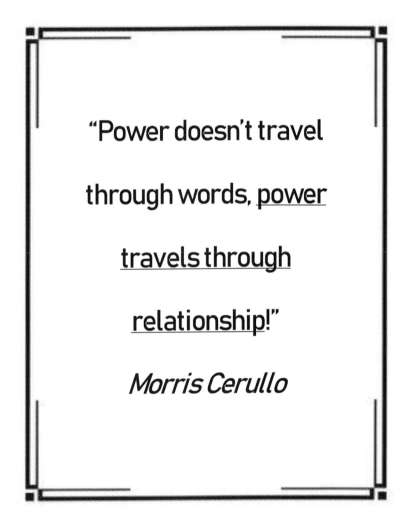

"Power doesn't travel through words, <u>power travels through relationship!</u>"

Morris Cerullo

CHAPTER
SIX

GOD WILL STEADY YOU!

'I will steady him with My hand..." (Psalms 89:21 NLT)

Joel Osteen once said, "If you are not scared, then it's probably not your destiny!"

If we are comfortable all the time, we cannot reach our destiny.

To take new ground you will have to get out of your comfort zone.

When you let God meet you and bring you out of hiding from behind the baggage of fear, insecurity, lack, excuses, comparison, thinking little of our self, weakness, betrayal, hurt, failure, even success – and you say yes to Him and to His great destiny that is bigger than you, God has a great promise...

Not only will He remind you that He found you, and that He anointed you, and that it was He that began and will complete this good work in you, as you step in to your promotion, God told David...

I will steady you with My hand! *(Psalms 89:21)*

He did not promise that David would not face battles with himself, with his enemies and even with his friends along the way as he stepped in to God's great promotion for his life.

But God did promise that in the midst of his challenges, his fears, his insecurities, his battles, his disappointments, his betrayals, and even his failures, that He would be with David to steady him with His hand and strengthen him with His mighty arm, and take him to his destiny!

It is not God's will for you to live in struggle mode – stress mode – anxiety mode – as you step into your promotion...

Proverbs 17:27 NKJV says *"...a man of understanding is of a calm spirit."*

There is a calming, steadying hand that God wants to stretch out over your life, if you will come under His hand...

God's hand is stretched out to steady you today as He takes you to your promotion...

God's hand is upon you to steady you <u>as He takes you from being an echo to being a voice</u>...

God's hand is upon you to steady you <u>as He takes you from merely getting a blessing to being a blessing</u>,

Or as Dr. Cerullo says, God's hand is stretched out to steady you as He takes you "<u>PAST the point of BLESSING and into an experience of His POWER</u>..."

John Maxwell says success is adding value to yourself; significance is adding value to others...

God's hand is upon you to steady you as He takes you from success to significance...

When God's steadying hand is upon you, you will step into your promotion WITHOUT COMMOTION!

But here was the game changing key for David and here is the breakthrough key for you and me:

In order for God's steadying hand to be upon you, you need to be near God's presence to be UNDER the hand of God!

In other words, you cannot expect to have Saturday night fever and receive Sunday morning favor!

Remember, "God's Power doesn't travel through words, God's power travels through relationship!" – Morris Cerullo

The seven sons of Sceva were in for a rude awakening when they discovered that God's power does not travel by echoing someone else's words – or copying someone else's powerful ministry – without having your own relationship and experience with God...

"A group of Jews was traveling from town to town casting out evil spirits. <u>They tried to use the name of the Lord Jesus in their incantation, saying, "I command you in the name of Jesus, whom Paul preaches, to come out!"</u> Seven sons of Sceva, a leading priest, were doing this.

<u>*But one time when they tried it, the evil spirit replied, "I know Jesus, and I know Paul, but who are you?"*</u> *Then the man with the evil spirit leaped on them, overpowered them, and attacked them with such violence that they fled from the house, naked and battered.*" (Acts 19:13-16 NLT)*

Here is a great truth: <u>EVERY BLESSING OF GOD IS TIED TO CONNECTION AND RELATIONSHIP WITH HIM</u>.

<u>The greatest investment you or I can make in our life is spending time with God and in His Word</u>.

Time with God is not an obligation. <u>It is an opportunity</u> with a great reward...

Your life – your family – your destiny – your finances... Your promotion from God - is 100% tied to your investment in your relationship with God...

Hebrews 11:6b KJV says, ***"God is a REWARDER of those that diligently seek Him!"***

<u>Our relationship with God is not based on obligation, it is based on opportunity</u>.

Fasting more is not an obligation, it is an opportunity...

Reading God's word more is not an obligation, it is an opportunity...

Praying more is not an obligation, it is an opportunity...

Giving more is not an obligation, it is an opportunity...

God is a responder...

"Oh, that we might know the Lord! Let us press on to know Him. He will respond to us as surely as the arrival of dawn or the coming of rains in early spring." (Hosea 6:3 NLT)

You are as close to God as you choose to be.

Over one year ago, during this season of promotion, God challenged me not to get out of bed in the morning before I spent time in His word.

I explained to God that unlike my always-cheerful wife Jeri, I am not a morning person! I told God that the afternoon or the evening were better times for me...

God reminded me of His word, and the opportunity He was presenting for those that put Him first in their day, ***"Seek ye FIRST the kingdom of God, and His righteousness, and all these things will be added to you" (Matthew 6:33 KJV)***

My You Version Bible app tells me that today is my 370th consecutive day of being in God's Word first thing in the morning. I have never been closer to Him. I have never heard His voice as I now hear His voice. My fears have been steadied. My marriage and my family and my finances have been blessed as never before. <u>A desire that became a discipline has now become a delight</u>...

Jacob was at a defining moment of greater destiny and promotion when he realized that he didn't have what he needed to take his next step. He had done well up to this point in his own strength and with the favor of God upon his life. He was blessed. But Jacob needed something more...

He needed God to break the greatest fear in his life so he could step into his promotion. He was about to face his brother Esau, who he was sure wanted to kill him. He got alone with God and determined that he would not let Him go until He changed him and his circumstances.
(Genesis 32:26)

He pursued God with passion. He wasn't depending on a formula, and he wasn't just looking for a blessing. He was determined to make a greater connection and have a fresh experience with the God that called him and chose him and spoke destiny over his life 20 years earlier in Bethel...

Because Jacob decided to make a stronger connection with God, God powerfully responded to Jacob's encounter...

"Your name will no longer be Jacob...from now on you will be called Israel..." **(Genesis 32:28 NLT)**

All the powerful promises of Psalms 91 – freedom from fear – victory over the traps of the enemy – angelic intervention – no plague coming to your home or your family – answered prayer – deliverance – power - honor – increase – health – long life -- promotion –<u>all these promises are not just tied to confessing them, they are tied to making connection and relationship with God a priority</u>...

"He that dwelleth in the secret place of the Most High shall abide <u>under the shadow</u> of the Almighty. (You can't be under His shadow unless you are NEAR Him!!)
I will say of the Lord, He is <u>my refuge</u> and <u>my fortress</u>, my God <u>in Him will I trust</u>. Surely, he shall deliver thee from the snare of the fowler, and from the noisome pestilence. He shall cover thee with <u>His feathers</u>, and <u>under His wings</u> shalt thou trust, His truth shall be they

90

shield and buckler. Thou shalt not be afraid for the terror by night or the arrows that flieth by day; Nor for the pestilence that walketh in the darkness...there shall be no evil befall thee, neither shall any plague come nigh thy dwelling. For he shall give His angels charge over thee, to keep thee in all thy ways...Because he has set his love upon Me, therefore will I deliver him; I will set him on high because he has known my name. He shall call upon me and I will answer him; I will be with him in trouble; I will deliver him and honor him. With long life will I satisfy him and show him my salvation!" (Psalms 91:1-6a, 10-11, 14-16 KJV)

Isaiah 26:3 NKJV says, *"God will keep in perfect peace, whose mind is stayed on Him."*

When God has our attention and our thoughts are on Him, then we have the promise of His perfect peace. All His promises are based on connection and relationship. God created us and our destiny to be blessed and to prosper based on relationship with Him.

Webster's Dictionary says a promotion is *an upgrade, an advancement, an elevation, an ascent*.

<u>The greatest promotion will be the upgrade you make in your relationship – your connection – your priority – your time – with your God</u>.

To step into our divine destiny, you and I will need to do what Jacob did. He decided to upgrade and elevate his connection and relationship with the God who found him, called him and anointed him, so that he could step into God's ability to fulfill God's greater destiny for his life…

As you do, God's powerful, calming, peaceful, steadying hand will be upon you!

Now we are ready to look at the key to it all – the final, glorious seventh promotion promise of God: <u>The God that will strengthen you with His mighty arm</u>...

Your fears will not

be fulfilled

and your hopes

shall be granted!

Proverbs 10:24

CHAPTER
SEVEN

GOD WILL MAKE YOU STRONG IN THE BATTLE!

"With My powerful arm I will make him strong..."

(Psalms 89:21b NLT)

Thirty God breathed words found in Psalms 89:20-21, where God celebrates His sovereign dealing with David, concludes with a great and powerful promise, "with My powerful arm I will make Him strong!"

"I have found my servant David...

I have anointed him with My holy oil...

I will steady him with My hand...

<u>With My powerful arm, I will make Him strong"</u>

God set the example when He expects that we not think little of ourselves. One thing that is clear when we read these two verses and the entire Bible is that God is not a God who thinks little of Himself or His abilities!

When we read the thirty words of Psalms 89:20-21, God refers to Himself eight times and David four times. It is also clear that in God's view, He had everything to do with finding, anointing, steadying and strengthening David. God was not depending on anything that David possessed. God was depending on what He could make of him.

God celebrated Himself. David and his promotion were the object of His celebration...

God is celebrating Himself even as you read these words.

You and your promotion are the object of His celebration!

We have been on a journey through these pages to indeed discover that your promotion is in motion...

We learned that God encouraged you to come out of hiding from your promotion. Then He reminded you not to think little of yourself, nor to allow your mistakes to define, disqualify or hold you back.

Then God reminded you that He initiated His great plan and purpose for you when He found you, He chose you, and anointed you with His holy oil.

Which brings us to where you are right now...you are stepping out of your comfort zone and out of your fear and into the greater purpose, promotion and reward of God for your life.

In his message "Scared To Greatness", Joel Osteen said, "On the other side of fear is a destiny bigger than you can imagine. If you weren't afraid, it wouldn't be your destiny.

We are at our best when we are a little uncomfortable because healthy fear will cause you to depend on God!"

Joshua was about to step into his promotion. Moses was dead. It was Joshua's time to lead. God spoke a word supercharged with encouragement directly to Joshua and to his fears to remind him that like David, God's hand would steady him, and His mighty arm would strengthen him:

"No one will be able to stand against you as long as you live. For I will be with you as I was with Moses. I will not fail you or abandon you. Be strong and courageous for you are the one that will lead these people...Be strong and very courageous...STUDY THIS BOOK OF INSTRUCTION CONTINUALLY. Meditate on it day and night, so you will be sure to obey everything written in it. Only then, will you prosper and succeed in all you do. This is My command – Be Strong and Courageous! Do not be afraid or discouraged for the Lord your God is

with you wherever you go." (Joshua 1:5-9 NLT) This scripture is framed and on my desk.

God encouraged Joshua to make one of the greatest investments he could make to walk in the strength and fearlessness he would need to successfully step into his promotion: Study this book of instruction continually... to prioritize daily time studying and meditating on the Word of God: **"Only then will you prosper and succeed in all you do..."** **(Joshua 1:8b NLT)**

Increasing and upgrading your study time in the Word of God is not an obligation but it is a great opportunity for you to receive a greater impartation of God's strength to feed your future and starve your fears...

When Jesus was confronted by Satan as it was time for His ministry to manifest - and it was His time to step into His promotion, Jesus identified the power and priority of the Word of God as the source of His strength when He faced the voice of the Accuser and quoted the scripture as He resisted the devil, *"Man shall not live by bread alone, but by every word that proceeds from the mouth of God!" (Matthew 4:4 NKJV)*

Although Jesus was the Word, as a man He set an example of being an incredible student of the Word of God.

Jesus began His ministry declaring Isaiah 61:1-2, referred to the scriptures hundreds of times during His ministry, and even breathing His last breath on the cross, quoted from Psalm 27.

If Jesus needed to meditate daily in the Word, how can we not? Daily time in the Word is the greatest investment you can make in setting a strong foundation in your life and in your destiny – and establishing the voice of God as the greatest voice in your life.

God told David, "With My powerful arm I will make you strong…"

How can you receive the same strength that David received, that Joshua received, that Gideon received, that Samuel received, that Sarah received, that Abraham received, that all the great men and woman of faith featured in the Hebrews 11 "Hall of Faith" received to step into their destinies?

Their powerful secret is found in Hebrews 11:33-34 NLT, **"By faith these people overthrew kingdoms, ruled with justice, and received what God had promised them…Their weakness was turned to strength. THEY BECAME _STRONG IN BATTLE_ and put whole armies to flight!"**

They did not become strong in their comfort zone…

They did not become strong focusing on their fears…

They did not become strong talking about it...

They did not become strong sitting on the sidelines...

Hebrews 11:34 declares, "***By faith their weakness was turned to strength***..."

THEY BECAME STRONG IN THE BATTLE!

Every man and every woman that God has ever used had weaknesses that in the hands of God would need to be turned to strength. None of these great men and women of the Bible were super heroes, they were flawed, imperfect, fearful, unqualified, flesh and blood – just like you and me – that decided they would not run FROM the battle, but with God, they would run TO the battle...

Your promotion is in motion. Now is God's time for you to move from the sidelines and get back in the game...

Your setback is not your set aside or your set down –
your setback is God's set up for your COMEBACK and
your comeback begins now because your promotion is
still in motion!

God will make you strong IN the battle...in the place of
your promotion.

When God created Adam He also created a place of
destiny for Adam...

"Then the Lord God formed the man from the dust of the
ground...then the Lord God planted a garden in Eden in
the east, and there he placed the man He had made"
(Genesis 2:7-8 NLT)

Your legacy and God's greatest blessing are waiting in the
place that God has created for you.

You still have significant destiny to fulfill...

Your promotion may be wrapped up in the thing you fear...but God will turn your weakness to strength, and you will become strong when you run to your promotion and not from it...

David's promotion was wrapped up in Goliath. He became strong as he ran toward his fear...

I will never forget the day I was in my hotel room, preparing to preach and minister that night when the voice of God rocked me to my core as I was reading Proverbs 10:24 NLT, *"The fears of the wicked will be fulfilled, the hopes of the godly will be granted."*

As I read those words, I heard the Lord's voice boom on the inside and say, "Greg, **YOUR FEARS WILL NOT BE FULFILLED AND YOUR HOPES SHALL BE GRANTED!"**

Unhealthy fear is a lie...

I declare that your fears WILL NOT be fulfilled, and your hopes shall be granted...

The Lord will turn your weakness into strength, and He will strengthen you as you step IN to your promotion.

Jeri and I experienced an unusual manifestation of the favor of God during the past several weeks as I wrote this book. (Although the book only took a few weeks to write, it was based on prayer and notes I had organized from nearly a year of my own experience, study and preparation).

Those of you that know me will know two things about me. I am a big man and I fly a lot. According to American Airlines, I have flown over 2.1 million miles. As a platinum with American, very occasionally Jeri and I will be offered an upgrade from coach to first class. Since American merged with US Air a few years ago, and merged both of their frequent flyer programs, upgrades are even fewer and far between, maybe once or twice a year maximum we will be offered an upgrade to first class.

During the past several weeks, we had three occasions to fly. They were not short flights. I used my time on each of these flights to write this book. Without fail, twenty-four hours before <u>each of these</u> flights I received an email from American with the most glorious subject line, "Your Upgrade Is Confirmed!"

A promotion is an upgrade...

It was as if God was confirming not just to me but to those that would read this book, "Your promotion is in motion and your upgrade is confirmed!"

God chose you. God anointed you. God is steadying you with his hand and with His powerful Arm He is making you strong...

Heaven is waiting...

The world is waiting...

Now is your time to step into your destiny, because the Lord is with you, your upgrade is confirmed and YOUR PROMOTION IS IN MOTION!